The Wonderful World
Coloring Book

The
Wonderful World
Coloring Book
Immerse yourself in these delightful images

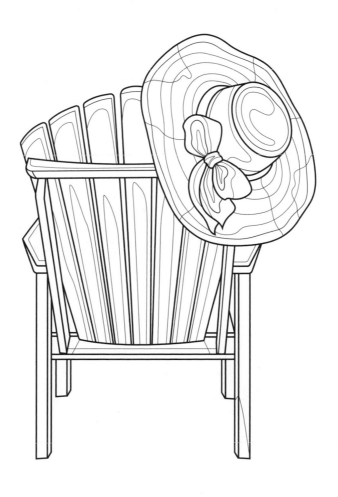

SIRIUS

SIRIUS

This edition published in 2024 by Sirius Publishing, a division of
Arcturus Publishing Limited,
26/27 Bickels Yard, 151–153 Bermondsey Street,
London SE1 3HA

ISBN: 978-1-3988-3703-4
CH011158NT
Supplier 29, Date 1123, PI 00005131

Printed in China

Introduction

What makes your world wonderful? Is it travel to new places, a countryside walk, or a visit to your favorite big city? Or is it a slice of sumptuous gateau, an ice cream in the sunshine, or a perfectly done hamburger and fries? Or paddling in a boat that leaves from its own private lakeside mooring or cycling on a summer's day? Or settling down with a beloved pet, a kitten maybe, or a soulful dog? This delightful coloring book is packed with images that will make you smile or evoke a special time. Whether your world centers on your garden or you love to remember a glorious vacation spent on glamorous Mediterranean shores, or sailing on a vintage tall ship, there will be an artwork that you'll want to color in these pages. Take a selection of pencils, pens or markers, find your peaceful place and color your cares away.

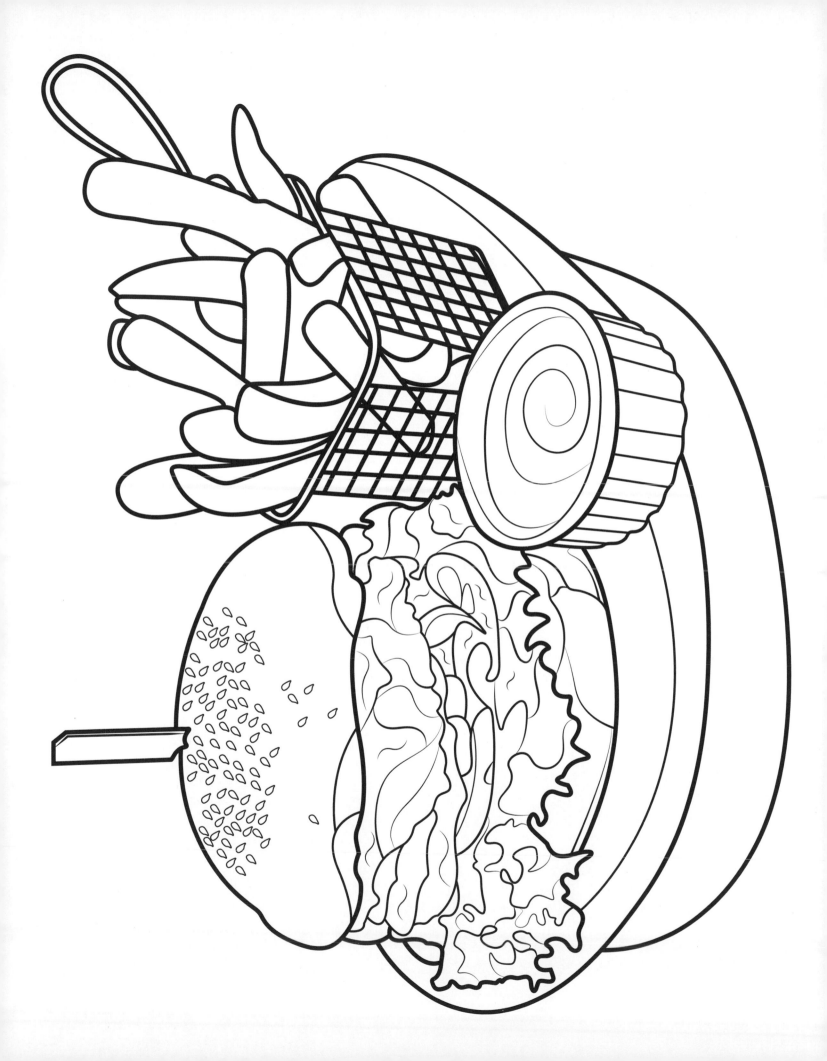